The Deep Blue Planet

THE CORAL REEF

Beautiful panorama of the coral reef at Hurghada, Egypt, on the Red Sea. In the foreground, a masked butterflyfish (*Chaetodon semilarvatus*); in the background, a school of Suez fusiliers (*Caesio suevicus*).

The Deep Blue Planet

THE CORAL REEF

RENATO MASSA
ENGLISH TRANSLATION BY LINDA SERIO

RSVP

RAINTREE
STECK-VAUGHN
PUBLISHERS
The Steck-Vaughn Company

Austin, Texas

Published by Raintree Steck-Vaughn Publishers, an imprint of Steck-Vaughn Company

Editors
Caterina Longanesi, Linda Zierdt-Warshaw, William P. Mara

Design and layout
Jaca Book Design Office

Library of Congress Cataloging-in-Publication Data

Massa, Renato.
    [La barriera corallina. English]
    The coral reef / Renato Massa ; English translation by Linda Serio.
        p.   cm. — (The deep blue planet)
    Includes bibliographical references (p.52) and index.
    Summary: Presents an in-depth examination of the basic composition of life found in the coral reef environment.
    ISBN 0-8172-4652-5
    1. Coral reef ecology — Juvenile literature.   [1. Coral reef ecology.   2. Ecology.]
I. Title.   II. Series.
QH541.5.C7M37   1998
577.7'89 — dc21   96–40488
                                                                         CIP   AC

Printed and bound in the United States
1 2 3 4 5 6 7 8 9 0   WO   01 00 99 98 97

Picture Credits

Photographs
GIANNI ARCUDI, Bergamo: 8 , 18-19, 24-25, 26 (3), 37 (6), 28-29, 32-33, 34-35, 37, 38-39. EDITORIALE JACA BOOK, Milano (GIORGIO DETTORI): 45; (RENATO MASSA): 12. GRANATA PRESS, Milano (IFA): 22; (KORD): 15 (2); (DAN LEE): 14 (1). GRAZIA NERI, Milano (H. BAMBERGER): 44; (THOMAS IVES): 21 (2, 4); (JONES-SHIMLOCK) 21 (3); (J. LANGEVIN): 47; (LOS ALAMOS NATIONAL LABORATORY/SCIENCE PHOTO LIBRARY): 46; (AYMAN S. TAMER): 43; (NORBERT WU): 20-21 (1). STEFANIA NOSOTTI, Milano: 17, 23, 26 (1, 2), 27 (4, 5, 7, 8). FOLCO QUILICI: 42 (2).

Color plates and drawings
EDITORIALE JACA BOOK, Milano (TIZIANO GIULIANINI): 42; (MARIA ELENA GONANO): 10-11, 12-13, 16-17, 48-49; (GIULIA RE): 8, 14, 15, 18-19, 30-31, 36, 37, 40-41.

CONTENTS

Introduction 9

Birth of a Coral Reef 10

Tiny Reef Builders 16

The Australian Barrier Reef Pools 22

The Fishes 28

Mutual Aid Societies 34

Poisonous Life in the Reef 36

Sharks 38

The Future of the Reef 42

Glossary 50

Further Reading 52

Index 53

Please note: words in **bold** can also be found in the glossary. They are bold only the first time they appear in the main body of the text.

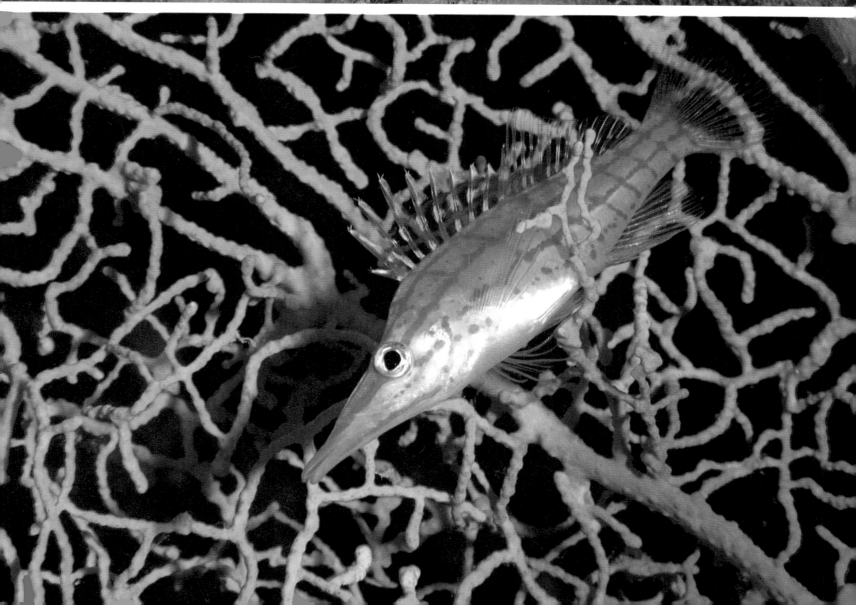

INTRODUCTION

The oceans and seas are wondrous places of both dark and light, flora and fauna, warm and cold, and life and death. Many regions are still largely unknown to us, so there is little doubt that hundreds of mysteries still lie in their murky depths.

The oceans and seas cover just over 70 percent of the Earth. They have provided us with many pieces to the puzzle of how life began on this planet, since the earliest forms of life were thought to have existed there. The rocks and sediment along the ocean floor have yielded a great deal of fossil evidence over the years.

The value of the oceans and seas is immeasurable. They have given us many useful chemicals and minerals, including bromine, magnesium, and salt, not to mention pearls for jewelry and shells for building material and health supplements. Most experts believe we have not yet realized their full potential in regard to nutrition, though it is believed that humans derive at least 10% of their overall protein from the Earth's waters, either directly or indirectly. Finally, there is the recreational aspect. Activities such as swimming, fishing, boating, diving, and so on, when executed properly and responsibly, provide us with a great deal of pleasure and a measure of relief from the grind of our daily lives.

Sadly, however, we humans have caused some serious damage to the oceans and seas in recent times. Industry is the greatest violator, with over a quarter of a million manufacturing facilities using the great bodies of water as dumping grounds for their often highly dangerous waste products, including mercury, lead, sulfuric acid, and asbestos. In addition, towns and cities regularly dump improperly treated sewage and millions of tons of paper and plastic wastes into rivers, streams, and lakes. Plastics in particular have the potential to remain intact for hundreds of years.

However, we have not yet reached a point of no return, and one of the goals of the *Deep Blue Planet* books is to give you a deeper understanding of—and in turn a deeper appreciation and respect for—the aquatic environments of this world. The more you know about any subject, the greater your appreciation for it will be, and the oceans and seas are in desperate need of increased appreciation. Perhaps someday you will make efforts of your own to preserve these beautiful natural areas and the myriad life forms that thrive within them. If so, you will be helping to guarantee them the bright and vibrant future they so richly deserve.

BIRTH OF A CORAL REEF

Against the backdrop of a Pacific atoll, the physical and biological elements (**1, 2, 3, 4**) that decide the birth of a coral reef are illustrated. Sections **a, b, c,** and **d** above and their corresponding aerial views (**a, b, c,** and **d** below) show phases of this birth. Physical and biological conditions:
1. A water temperature of no more than 26° C (78°F) is required. Such temperatures exist with any kind of regularity only in tropical seas. **2.** The water must be clear. Such waters are far from river deltas or other sources of murkiness. **3.** Organisms that can build a reef are needed. These include the Anthozoan cnidarians of the madrepores. **4.** Last, volcanic activity must have created an island, which gradually sank into the sea.
The phases of birth are probably those suggested by Charles Darwin in his article on the subject in 1842. **a.** During a sudden eruption, a volcanic island emerges in the open sea. **b.** As time passes, a new coastline forms around the island. Clear, shallow shoals allow the survival of madrepores, which multiply in ever-spreading colonies. **c.** Because of a settling effect known as subsidence, the island begins to sink into the sea at a rate of a few centimeters (in) each year. The sinking carries the coral into deeper, murkier waters. This causes the madrepore colony to die. The colony would be forever extinct if polyps did not continue to build new thecas upon the mass of coral skeletons that have gathered over time. The calcareous skeletons of millions of dead madrepores gather on top of each other. This endless layering keeps the colony in water shallow enough to ensure its survival. **d.** Finally, the volcanic base of the island disappears into the sea, and the coral atoll that covers it remains.

The Very Large and the Very Tiny

On our planet, very large objects and very tiny ones exist side by side. Many of these objects share close relationships. Such relationships are seen among the rocky parts of some of the most impressive mountain ranges in the world.

The Dolomite Alps are located in northeastern Italy. Here, at altitudes of thousands of meters (ft), are the fossil remains of tiny organisms. These remains began changing the landscape as far back as the Triassic Period, which occurred about 240 million years ago.

1

During the Triassic, the land now occupied by the Dolomite Alps was covered by a warm ocean. This ocean has since been named the Tethys. The clear, warm water at the land's edges swarmed with creatures that had skeletons and shells made up of calcium compounds. These creatures, commonly called coral, are also known as **madrepores**.

The madrepores lived together in large groups. Together they formed structures that grew in the shallow waters. Over time, these structures formed coral **reefs**. Similar structures are seen today in the warm waters of

the Red Sea and off the eastern coast Australia.

Like all living things, madrepores died the end of their **life cycles**. Their hard skel tal remains gathered, layer upon layer, at t bottom of the sea. For millions of years, t sea floor gradually sank. At the same tin madrepore remains built up. The remai formed a constantly growing structure. T

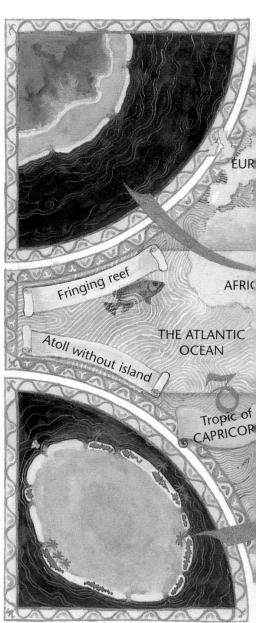

top of this structure stayed near the wate surface, and new generations of madrepor lived atop this structure. They continued grow near the water's surface, a conditic necessary for the survival of the species.

The Origin of the Dolomites

As time passed, the waters of the Teth became murky, and the madrepores died o

They were covered by sediments that formed a crust that protected their remains. The sediments were made mostly of marl, a crumbly rock similar to clay.

Over time, geological forces raised the area where the Dolomites now stand. The old and new rocky formations also became raised. The region rose up from beneath the water, reaching heights far above sea level.

which these mountains are made, into the sea. There, the calcium bicarbonate in the limestone is recycled. It becomes available again to a variety of marine organisms that use the calcium to form new skeletons and shells.

1. A view of the northern calcareous (limestone) Alps in Switzerland. This is one of the many chains of sedimentary rock that shows the effects of madrepore construction.

2. The global arrangement of coral reefs shown in bands of lighter colors. In the four corners are diagrams of different reef types. FRINGING REEFS, also known as

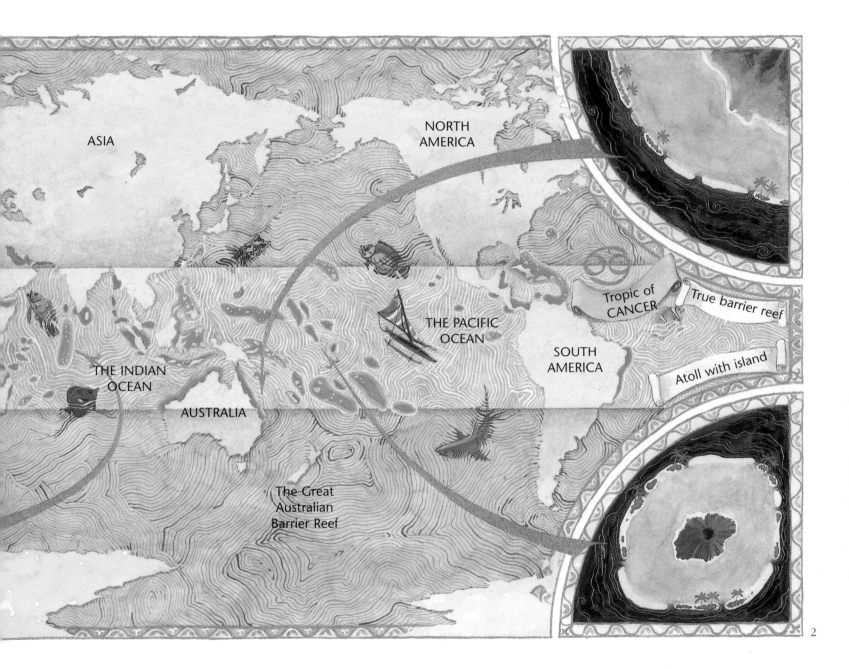

No longer covered by the sea, the marly crust was eroded by wind and rain. Over time, the **calcareous** (containing calcium carbonate) core was exposed, and the range now called the Dolomites was born.

Today the sunset paints the walls and peaks of the Dolomites dazzling shades of pink. Rain, snow, and ice slowly erode these mountains. Rivers carry the **limestone**, from

COASTAL REEFS, emerge along coastlines, continental edges, and around islands. ATOLLS are reefs that emerge around volcanic islands that may or may not have sunk into the sea. TRUE BARRIER REEFS extend far from the coastline, along the edges of the continental shelf, or around partly submerged islands.

1. An aerial view of the Great Barrier Reef of Australia. It is the largest madrepore structure on Earth and is visible even from space. Extending for about 2,000 kilometers (1200 mi) along the northeastern coast of Australia, the reef has a surface area of approximately 349,000 square kilometers (135,000 square mi). **2.** Green Island, Great Barrier Reef, northern Queensland, Australia. **3.** Section of a model coral reef. The inner part, described as leeward or lagoonward, appears left. The outer windward, or seaward, part appears right. Moving from the open sea to the inside of the reef is a ridge. It rises as much as 50 centimeters (20 in) beyond the base. The ridge remains covered by water even during low tide. Beyond the ridge, a deeper area known as the moat begins. Strong currents from the open sea flow over the ridge, bringing well-oxygenated water to this area. Next, the reef flat begins. It may be followed by a small madrepore islet and the lagoons where the greatest coral density exists. **4.** Profile of the outer slope of a reef dropping to a depth of about 100 meters (330 ft). Boulder coral grows on the seaward side. It resists the force of waves breaking against the reef. A cavern and madrepores to a maximum depth of 90 meters (300 ft) are also present.

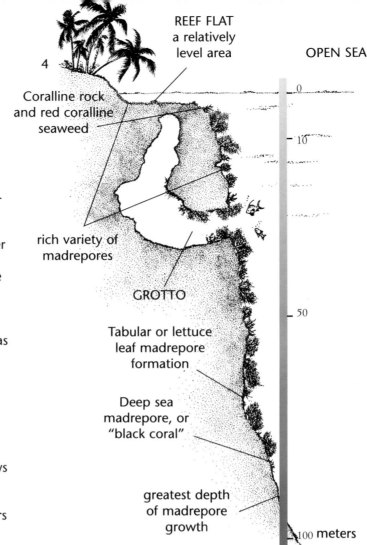

REEF FLAT
a relatively
level area

OPEN SEA

4

0

10

Coralline rock
and red coralline
seaweed

rich variety of
madrepores

GROTTO

50

Tabular or lettuce
leaf madrepore
formation

Deep sea
madrepore, or
"black coral"

greatest depth
of madrepore
growth

100 meters

1

ISLAND

sand and
mud

2

INTERNAL
LAGOON
(cloudy)

KNOLL
pinnacle

EXTERNAL
LAGOON
(clear)

leeward or
lagoonward
side

windward or
seaward side

direction of the
dominant winds

REEF
FLAT

RIDGE

REEF
FLAT

MOAT

TERRACE

OPEN SEA

madrepores

madrepores

3

madrepores

mud

FINE
SAND

INTERNAL
SLOPE

CORAL
ISLE

TIDAL
CHANNEL

SLOPE

50

100

gorgonians
and sponges

150
meters

Tiny Reef Builders

Polyps Upon Polyps

The building process of a reef or **atoll** takes many years. A coral reef is a tropical marine **ecosystem**. This ecosystem includes thousands of species. The part of the reef that gives rise to atolls and mountains is made up of solid limestone.

The limestone of a reef is formed mostly by one group of organisms—the aforementioned madrepores. Madrepores are a type of colonial **cnidarian**. Cnidarians are animals that have a sac-like body and stinging cells. These stinging cells are called **nematocysts**.

The calcareous construction of a reef resembles hardened plants. It is made up of a series of cup-like skeletal **thecas**. Within the thecas, an unusual **colony** of organisms lives and grows. In this colonial relationship, each individual is connected to every other.

Cnidarians are the simplest multi-celled organisms of modern-day Earth. They differ from sponges and protozoans by their sac-like structure, which includes an inner cavity for digestion. The inner cavity is very simple. It opens directly to the outside and serves as both mouth and anus.

Because they have both a mouth and a digestive organ, cnidarians can take in food that is larger than that which is fed upon by protozoans and sponges. For example, sponges take in food directly through their cells. This ability causes some scientists to consider sponges to be colonies of single-celled instead of well-organized and multi-celled organisms.

All cnidarians have *tentacles* surrounding their mouths. The tentacles contain the aforementioned stinging cells. These stinging tentacles make it easier for a cnidarian to catch and take in food.

Because of their tentacles, many cnidarians can live anchored to a stable surface, such as the ocean floor. Such cnidarians (e.g., sea anemones and madrepores) are called **polyps**. The term *polyp* comes from the Latin *polypus*, meaning "many feet." A polyp also is a sessile (non-mobile) stage in the cnidarian life cycle. Some cnidarians live their entire lives as polyps. The madrepores, which belong to the class **Anthozoa**, are an example. Other cnidarians change between a sessile phase and a mobile phase. The mobile stage in the cnidarian life cycle is called a **medusa**. An example of cnidarians that live as medusas are the jellyfishes. The jellyfishes belong to the class **Scyphozoa**.

Colonies of Little Stingers

Anthozoa is the largest group of cnidarians. This group has about 6000 living species. They include the actiniids (sea anemones, order **Actiniae**), the gorgonians, and the madrepores.

Madrepores differ greatly from actiniids in appearance. However, the two groups are closely related. An important difference is the ability of madrepores to produce a calcium carbonate skeleton; actiniids do not produce such skeletons.

Some madrepores live on their own. A few are polyps that reach a diameter of 25 centimeters (10 in). However, most madrepores live in colonies of tiny polyps. These polyps range from 1 to 3 millimeters (around 0.125 in) in diameter.

Polyps gather their food at night. They use their tiny **cilia** (hair-like structures) to create currents that carry organic matter, including many tiny living creatures, to their mouths. Once an organism is near the polyp's mouth, it is paralyzed or killed by the nematocysts.

The calcium carbonate skeleton of madrepores, the aforementioned theca, is a sort of cup. The polyp forms inside the theca. When madrepores live in colonies, the theca wall of each individual is connected to the thecas of nearby individuals. Thus, all individuals in a madrepore colony are connected by a layer of tissue. The tissue is an extension of the **gastrovascular cavity**, which carries out both digestion and circulation.

Nematocysts are exclusive to cnidarians. They are the same "weapons" that cause discomfort to anyone who steps on a jellyfish or a sea anemone. Nematocysts cover the

The madrepores are only one Anthozoan order. They are the most highly differentiated class of cnidarian. Other orders include the Scyphozoa (jellyfish) and Hydrozoa (hydras and medusas).
Another large group of sea animals with transparent bodies and long tentacles belongs to a closely related subphylum—the ctenophores.
The photo in the box shows two madrepores: above, *Acropora* sp. (staghorn coral); below, *Goniastrea* sp. (boulder coral). Besides those shown, there are many other madrepore forms.

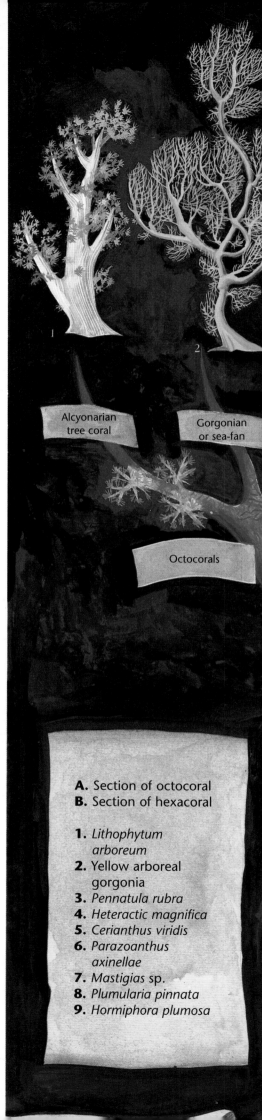

Alcyonarian tree coral

Gorgonian or sea-fan

Octocorals

A. Section of octocoral
B. Section of hexacoral

1. *Lithophytum arboreum*
2. Yellow arboreal gorgonia
3. *Pennatula rubra*
4. *Heteractic magnifica*
5. *Cerianthus viridis*
6. *Parazoanthus axinellae*
7. *Mastigias* sp.
8. *Plumularia pinnata*
9. *Hormiphora plumosa*

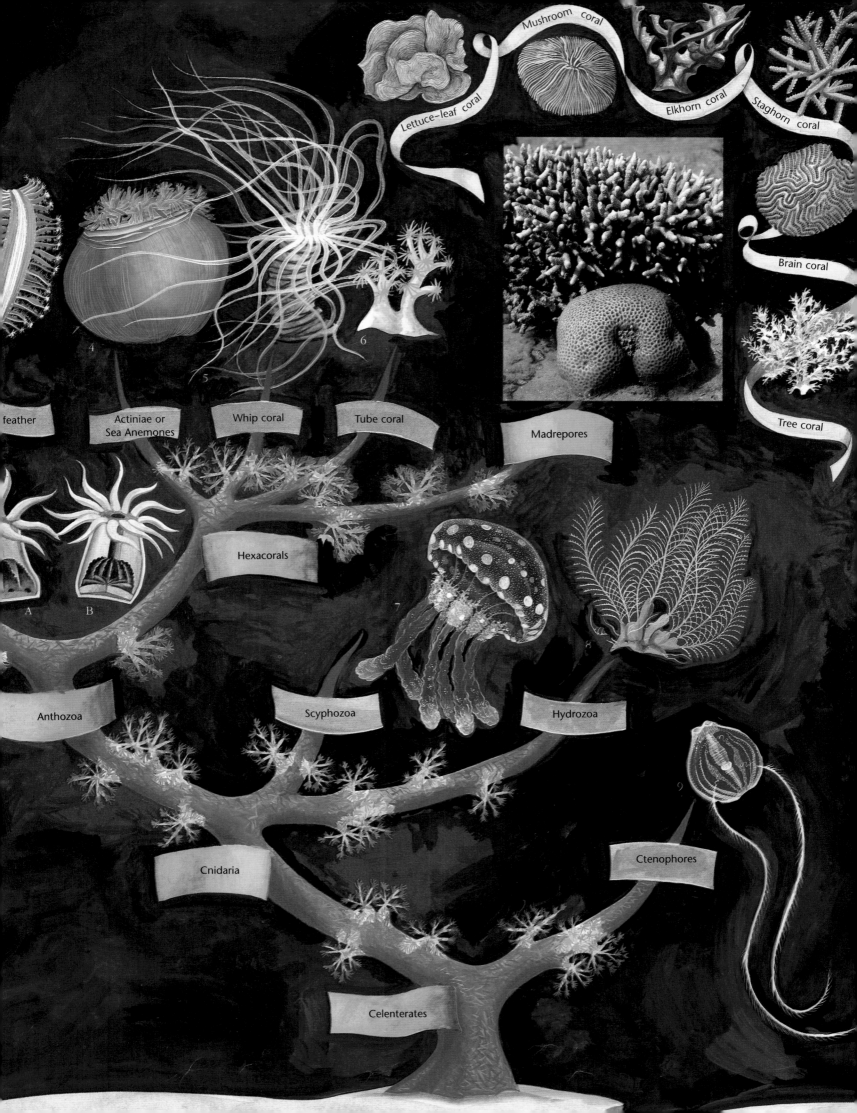

Mushroom coral

Lettuce-leaf coral

Elkhorn coral

Staghorn coral

Brain coral

feather

Actiniae or
Sea Anemones

Whip coral

Tube coral

Madrepores

Tree coral

Hexacorals

A   B

Anthozoa

Scyphozoa

Hydrozoa

Cnidaria

Ctenophores

Celenterates

entire outer skin of a polyp. However, they are most numerous on the tentacles.

The outer shape of a madrepore skeleton is determined by how the colony grows and by the arrangement of its polyps. Some species develop flattened forms. Others have rounded forms that look like a human brain. Still others grow in an upright, branched pattern that resembles bushes or trees.

Most coral colonies grow through **asexual reproduction**, i.e., reproduction that requires only one parent. However, anthozoans can also reproduce sexually, which requires two parents. During **sexual reproduction**, larvae are formed. The larvae are free-swimming, and in time they will find new colonies. There they will settle and change in form, becoming polyps. Because these polyps are formed from two parents, their genetic traits are not identical to the other polyps in the reef.

Successful Symbiosis

Some madrepore species live in temperate waters. A few live in the icy waters of the Arctic and Antarctic. However, most prefer tropical seas. About 35 madrepore species live in the Caribbean; at least 200 live in Australia's Great Barrier Reef.

The great coral reefs grow only in clear, warm waters. These waters have a minimum temperature of 26°C (78°F). Thus, such reefs are located only in the tropics, between 30° north latitude and 30° south latitude.

Madrepores live in fairly shallow water, usually 20 to 50 meters (65 to 165 ft) deep. The deepest water in which these organisms can survive is 90 meters (300 ft). This depth restriction is due to the presence, in their tissues, of single-celled algae called **zooxanthellae**. These algae—just like all plants—need light for photosynthesis. Zooxanthellae share a symbiotic relationship with the madrepores in which the madrepores use the oxygen and sugar produced by the zooxanthellae.

Zooxanthellae speed the production of skeletal limestone in madrepores. They do this by bringing about a reaction that changes calcium bicarbonate ($Ca[HCO_3]_2$) into calcium carbonate ($CaCO_3$), water (H_2O), and carbon dioxide (CO_2). This reaction occurs as the algae remove carbon dioxide from the madrepores. The algae change this carbon dioxide into glucose (sugar) during photosynthesis.

The growth of the madrepores can be as much as 24 centimeters (9 in) each year. The energy used in this growth is much greater than the eating of plankton would allow. This explains why zooxanthellae are so important to the life of the madrepores.

Madrepore colonies can grow for millions of years. One layer forms over another, even when the ocean floor is slowly sinking. Colonies can also spread out to cover large surfaces. In this way they create a solid foundation that is rich in gullies. Thousands of animal species find refuge among the reef using the gullies as hiding places.

The calcium carbonate of a reef may be broken apart by **gastropod** mollusks, **polychaetous annelids**, and parrotfish. The parrotfish crush the reef into bits with their jaws. The reef pieces are then "glued" back together with bits of shell and sea urchin skeletons. This remodeling is carried out by organisms such as the red algae and members of the **Bryozoa**. These organisms cover the dead coralline mass, bind its particles, and slowly cement them together to form a base for a **coralline island**.

1. Through the lens you can see an enlargement of the zooxanthellae algae (in yellow) that live in symbiosis with madrepores.
2. Madrepores are hexacorals; their skeletons are divided in six parts. Shown is a cross-section of a polyp of the *Tubastrea* sp.
3. A formation of boulder coral through which a school of *Pseudanthias squamipinnis* swims.

1

1. A large and beautiful lettuce-leaf (*Montispora* sp.) madrepore colony in the shoals off the coast of the island of Sipadan, Borneo.

2. Detail of the brainlike appearance of *Diploria labyrinthiformis*, a madrepore of the western Caribbean.

3. Below, another "brain" coral (*Symphyl* sp.) next to a pink sponge, Papua New Guinea.

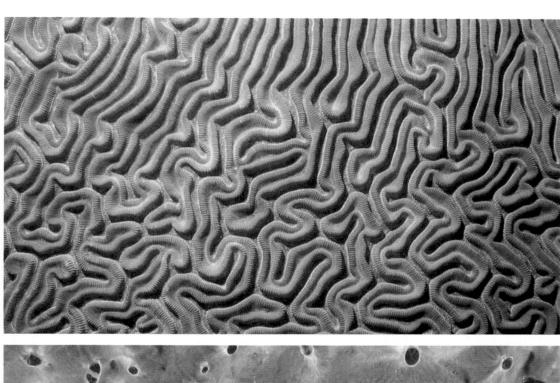

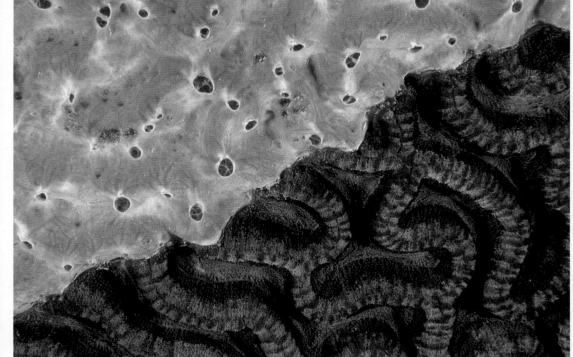

4. Detail of a boulder coral (*Montastrea
abernosa) upon which a small yellow
ponge grows, Caribbean Sea.

The Cays

The Great Barrier Reef is huge. It runs for 2000 kilometers (1200 mi) along the eastern coast of Australia. In total, the reef covers an area of 349,000 square kilometers (135,000 square mi).

Only a few peaks of reef rise above the water's surface, and these eventually are worn down by the action of the wind and the waves. This erosion results in flat coralline islands called **cays**. Cays are made up of fine particles and larger bits of madrepores. They stand slightly above the high tide line.

In Australia's Great Barrier Reef, there are approximately 70 cays of different sizes; enough to allow study of the traits and features that distinguish cays from other geological formations.

The Colorful Organisms of the Pool

The rocky coastline of a cay never completely dries, not even during low tide. It is always dotted with deep pools. Some stretches of rock appear soft and velvety. However, upon closer inspection, thousands of tiny polyp tentacles can be seen waving back and forth. More than 300 coral species live in the Great Barrier Reef, and this increases as one moves north toward warmer waters.

Among the madrepores, which seem to encrust everything, live intensely blue **sea stars**. Sea stars, which are often called starfish, move slowly across the bottom of a tidal pool. In spite of the sluggishness that gives them a somewhat "gentle" appearance, they are powerful predators. They can force open the shells of even the strongest **bivalves**. Many sea cucumbers—some a delicate purple, others dark green with red bumps—filter the coralline sand. Sea urchins also move slowly about. Polychaetous worms peek out from their tubular sheaths, showing off their refined crowns of gills.

The Strange Life of the Giant Clam

Approximately 4,000 mollusk species inhabit the Great Barrier Reef. Many of these are bivalves. Among the bivalves, the giant clam

1. Aerial view of the Great Australian Barrier Reef with its atolls emerging at low tide.
2. Stretch of an *Acropora* sp. madrepore uncovered during low tide, Great Barrier Reef, Australia.
3. A large brain-shaped madrepore formation of the *Symphyllia* sp.

23

(*Tridacna gigas)* deserves special attention. It is the grandest mollusk of all the tropical oceans. Its shell can reach a length of 1.3 meters (4.2 ft), and it may weigh as much as 200 kilograms (440 lbs). Its valves (shell halves) are so large, they often are used as holy water basins in churches.

The giant clam is known for its **symbiosis** with zooxanthellae. These algae supply the clam with oxygen for respiration. They also supply the clam with nutrients that are formed by their photosynthetic activity. As with the corals, the photosynthesis of the algae aids in the calcification, or hardening, of the mollusk's shell as the algae make use of the clam's wastes.

Blue, meaty tissue sticks out from both halves of the clam's closed shell. In this tissue, small and dark outgrowths can be seen. These growths act as lenses, allowing light to

2

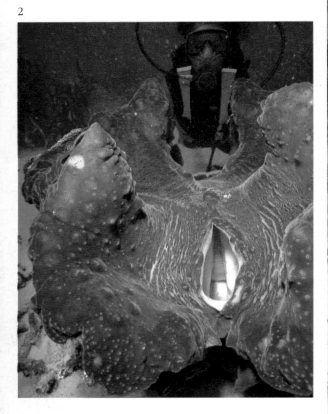

Two views of *Tridacna gigas,* a clam also known as the giant "holy water font."
1. Front view of a young clam and
2. the open valves of an adult. Between the valves are fleshy lips that fold inward. This allows algae in the clam to receive light.
In the deepest tissues of the clam—where algae are also found—the sunlight can penetrate thanks to crystalloid sacs in the clam's mantle. The sacs spread the light through the organism.

reach into the deeper tissues of the clam's **mantle**. The light supplies energy to the zooxanthellae living within the clam.

Since the giant clam depends on algae that depend on light, it lives only in clear, shallow water. In this water the clam anchors itself to coral rock. If the algae multiply too much, the clam absorbs them through its cells.

It may seem that the relationship between the giant clam and the zooxanthellae benefits only the clam (which in that case would not be true symbiosis). However, the algae benefit, too. First, they are protected from the sun's dangerous radiation by the blue, black, green, and brown pigments in the clam's mantle. They are also given a stable home. This home keeps them safe from the changes in temperature and pressure caused by the tides.

Some scholars define the Great Barrier Reef tidal pools as physiological "torture chambers;" this overstatement refers to the difficulties of surviving there. However, every reef creature has become well-suited to this habitat through millions of years of evolutionary development.

Among the many inhabitants of Australia's Great Barrier Reef are the madrepores.
1. Those of the genus *Acropora* make up a large part of the mineral mass of the reef. Well-known animals of the reef pools include the pale blue *Tridacna gigas*.
2. Among the gastropod mollusks are species of large sizes such as the spider shell (*Lambis lambis*). **3.** The sea floor is also dotted with sponges and **4.** and **5.** alcyonarian coral, *Sarcophyton* sp.
6. Here, with polyps retracted, are beautiful polychaetous annelids such as the *Spirobranchus gigantus*. **7.** The cyprea (*Ovula ovum*) gastropods are known for the beauty of their porcelain-white shells.
8. A vividly and unlikely colored sea star— *Linckia laevigata*.

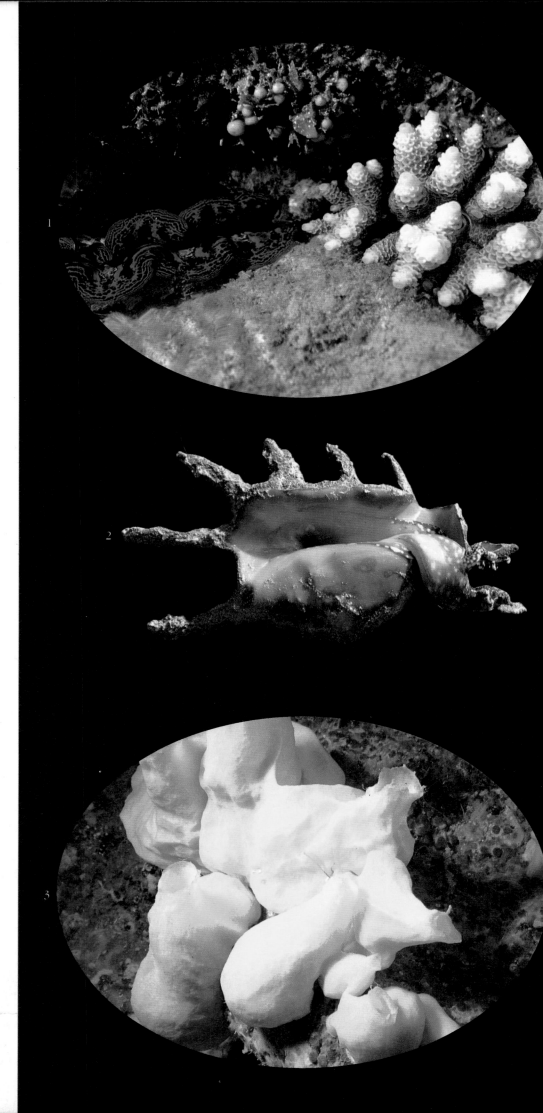

THE FISHES

Fish Paradise

The coral reef is truly a fish paradise, from both the fishes' and a human's point of view. Reef living conditions are very favorable for fishes. In fact, the many species crowding the reef reach a density of 2,000 kilograms per hectare (1,760 lbs per acre). The number of fishes living among coral reefs represents 30 percent of all the fish species that live in the oceans of the world. There are 1,500 different species in Australia's Great Barrier Reef alone.

The reef is a paradise for people, too. This paradise is created partly from the economic and scientific benefits of reefs. It also exists because of the exhibit it provides. Among the creatures of the reef are some of the most beautifully colored organisms on the planet. In the macroscopic (visible to the unaided eye) world, there are few creatures that compare to the fishes of the reef. The closest may be the magnificent birds and insects of the tropical rain forest.

Colorful Nametags

Within a reef environment, there is an amazing explosion of color. These colors are used to communicate. Often they are displayed on flattened bodies that, like billboards, offer large and easy-to-read surfaces.

The messages transmitted by color are very basic. For example, some fishes use color to identify themselves within groups of similar species. Members of the angelfish family (Pomacanthidae) are a good example. Some are yellow with a round black spot on each side, which is different from that of other fishes in the same family. Others may be yellow-and-black striped with a blue oval spot, yellow with blue spots, or yellow with black dots. Of course there are thousands of other possible designs as well. Fishes that recognize these colors can clearly identify an

angelfish, and those that want nothing to d with them or their territory know to sta away.

In an environment where there are no le than 1,800 species from 150 different fam lies, it is necessary for each species to be ea ily identifiable. And this is indeed demo strated by the vast variety of colors and pa terns possessed by the fishes of the India and western Pacific Oceans (where reefs a found) and those of the Atlantic and easter Pacific Oceans (which lack reefs). The India and western Pacific Oceans have a larg

3

1. French angelfish (*Pomacanthus paru*), Cuba. **2.** Sergeantfish (*Abudefduf* sp.) at the foot of a large gorgonian; right, a red encrusting sponge, the Red Sea. **3.** School of *Priacanthus hamrur*, the Seychelle Islands.

Following pages:
1. Yellow-striped triggerfish (*Balistapus undulatus*). **2.** French angelfish (*Pomacanthus paru*). **3.** Christmas Island angelfish (*Centropyge flavissimus*). **4.** Yellow-masked angelfish (*Pomacanthus xanthometopon*). **5.** Striped surgeonfish (*Acanthurus lineatus*). **6.** Parrotfish (*Scarus ferrugineus*). **7.** Merlet's scorpionfish (*Rhinopias aphanes*). **8.** Purple serranid (*Pseudanthias tuka*). **9.** Red-finned serranid (*Pseudanthias dispar*). **10.** Klunzinger's wrasse (*Thalassoma klunzingeri*) **11.** Lyretail (*Bodianus anthioides*). **12.** Long-nosed triggerfish (*Oxymonacanthus longirostris*). **13.** Seabat (*Platax pinnatus*). **14.** Bigeye (*Priacanthus hamrur*). **15.** Porcupinefish (*Diodon hystrix*).

mber of species that possess rich, striking lors than the Atlantic and eastern Pacific eans.

Varieties of Fishes in the Reef

tterfly fish (family Chaetodontidae) show f their colors to frighten enemies and ract mates. They can do this while living a world full of predators because of the ny hiding places the reef provides. These ding places also provide refuge for herbires, like some triggerfish, and the predars of tiny invertebrates, like the parrotfish.

Furthermore they allow different fishes to parade their colors without attracting too much attention from likely prey.

The fish of the Lutjanidae family, many members of the Serranidae family, and some of the slimy blennoids are colorful predators. The serranid *Epinephelus flavocoeruleus* may be up to 90 centimeters (35 in) in length. This fish is dark blue with bright yellow fins. *Plectropomus maculatus* is from the same family. It may be up to 95 centimeters (37 in) and weigh as much as 25 kilograms (55 lbs). It is a deep rose color with

blue, leopard-like spots. This design likely has a purpose since it is shared by three smaller serranids (*Variola louti*, *Cephalopholis miniata*, and *Cephalopholis aurantius*). These fishes are abundant from the Red Sea to Australia.

Warning Notice to All Fish

The bright colors of many fishes announce their potentially poisonous qualities. We say "potentially" because sometimes the warning colors are mere bluff, a way of tilting the odds in the favor of a harmless species while playing the great game of survival.

But again, sometimes the warning colors are worn by a fish that is very dangerous indeed. One example is the armored boxfish (of the family Ostraciidae). These fishes give off a poison that is strong enough to kill all inhabitants in close proximity. Fishes belonging to a closely related family are the puffers (family Tetraodontidae). The puffers include species whose meat is so poisonous, anyone who eats it may die. Puffers also have another protective feature—when threatened, they take in large amounts of water and swell greatly in size. By doing this, they reduce the risk of being swallowed.

Many puffers are brightly colored. This is not true of their close relatives the porcupinefish (family Diodontidae). Porcupinefish look much like puffers, and they also can "inflate" themselves to obscene sizes. Furthermore their bodies are covered with tough thorns. These thorns become even more dangerous when the fish are swollen.

Not all fishes have such elaborate methods of protection. One small fish, *Gnathypops rosenbergi*, simply digs a tunnel into the sea floor, then reinforces the walls of the tunnel with pieces of madrepore skeletons. Members of the pearlfish family (Carapidae) get food and shelter by moving into the bodies of other animals, such as sea cucumbers, clams, sea stars, sea urchins, and tunicates.

Long Faces, Tough Faces

Aside from not being eaten, it's also important to feed oneself as efficiently as possible. In the world of the coral reef there are many nooks and crannies, and a great deal of organic material (tiny animals, plant matter, etc.) finds its way into these places. To gather this for food, a fish must have a long and narrow snout. Thus, it is not surprising to

learn that this external characteristic h developed in many species. For example, it seen in several chaetodontids, some sigai dids (including the foxfish, *Lo vulpinu* and many zanclidids, such as the yello *Zebrasoma flavescens* and the strip *Zanclus canescens*.

Another long-snouted species is the tru petfish (*Aulostomus maculatus*). It tak advantage of the slenderness and opaq color of its body to attach itself to the bac of other fishes. It then waits for smaller fis es to come by while hoping to steal sor scraps of food from the host fish.

Triggerfishes and parrotfishes have ve strong jaws. They use these to cru madrepore skeletons and the shells of s urchins. This trait affords them access to virtual bounty of resources. To split open sea urchin of the *Diadem* genus, for exar ple, a triggerfish detaches bits of madrepo surrounding the sea urchin on the reef. Tł causes the reef to fall, and by creating a stro current of water, the triggerfish makes su its victim falls on its back. Then the triggerfi attacks the soft underparts of the urchin (t urchin's mouth, for instance, has no spine and proceeds to tear it up into small piece

1. Emperor angelfish (*Pomacanthus imperator*), the Red Sea. In many fish species of the reef, the color of the adult—while not always brighter—may differ from that of the young.
2. *Pseudanthias squamipinnis* against a background of madrepores, sponges, and soft coral, the Red Sea. These small (12 centimeter/4.5 in) serranids are among the most common inhabitants of coral reefs from eastern Africa to the Pacific. They live in social groups made up of several orange-tinted females and one bright red male. The male has a long, spiny appendage extending from his dorsal fin. Within a few

days of the male's death, the largest female changes her sex and replaces him. This socio-sexual organization is possible because these fish are hermaphrodites. They first develop their female reproductiv organs. Later, the male organs develop as the female organs disappear.
3. Hawkfish (*Oxycirrhitus typus*) among the elaborate branches c a gorgonian coral, Ras Mohame Red Sea. The long, pointed snou states that this is one of many predators that look for food in the narrow fissures and crannies that abound in the reef.

1

MUTUAL AID SOCIETIES

1. Cleaner shrimp (*Periclimenes pedersoni*) on a dappled grouper (*Epinephelus tauvina*), Grand Bahama Island, Bahamas. These shrimp set up cleaning stations much like the cleaner fish. They attract their "client's" attention by waving long white antennae that stand out against the color of their bodies.
2. A little goby (*Gobius ucchichii*), Red Sea. Like clownfish, gobies live in symbiosis with sea anemones.

3. Flamingo-tongue (*Ciphoma gibbosum*), a gastropod that is a dinner companion for bush or fan corals, Grand Cayman Islands, Caribbean Sea. The bright colors of the mollusk's mantle contrast those of the gorgonian. At first glance the gorgonian seems not to benefit from the mollusk.
4. Double-banded clownfish (*Amphiprion bincinctus*) on a sea anemone, Red Sea.
5. Another banded clownfish on a sea anemone (*Heractis magnifica*), Red Sea.
6. Clark's clownfish (*Amphiprion clarki*), from the Maldives.

Clownfish and Sea Anemones

Among the most notable traits of reef life are the symbiotic relationships that exist among its members. One of the best known of these exists between the sea anemone and the clownfish, which belongs to the genus *Amphiprion*.

Sea anemones, like all cnidarians, protect themselves with stinger cells. These cells are harmful to every animal *except* clownfish. The clownfish can swim through the tentacles of a sea anemone or hide among them with no ill effect to itself (or to the anemone, for that matter).

Experiments done in the 1950s by ethologist Irenaus Eibl-Eibesfeldt (an ethologist is a scientist who studies the behavior of animals) showed that clownfish have a coating of mucus that protects them from the harmful effects of an anemone's stingers by causing the anemone to confuse the fish with its own tentacles.

Although each species of clownfish produces a different mucus, the mucus protects them only from one or two anemone species.

Clownfish are born with the ability to produce this mucus. They are also born with the ability to recognize which species of sea anemone they may safely associate with.

The clownfish finds a useful refuge among anemones. It also provides several services to its host. For example, clownfish clean off parasites and defend anemones against any marine turtles that might feed on them. They perform this latter service by warning the turtles of the risk of being stung by the anemone's tentacles through the display of their own bright colors.

The variety of cardinalfish known as *Siphamia versicolor* shares a relationship with sea urchins that is similar to that of clownfishes and sea anemones. It hides within the thorny spines that protrude from a bed of sea urchins and also are dangerous to other species.

Cleaning Fish and False Cleaners

An interesting symbiosis exists between some small fishes and several large carnivorous fishes. The small fishes (e.g., *Labroides*

dimidiatus and *Elactinus oceanops*) are known as "cleaners." The larger fishes are usually groupers (e.g., *Epinephelus* spp.) and lutjanidids (e.g., *Plectorhinchus* spp.). The smaller fishes move close to the larger fishes and announce their arrival with a characteristic "dance." The larger fishes remain still during this performance, then open their mouths and their gills, allowing the small cleaner fishes to enter and look for parasites. The smaller fishes also pass over the entire surface of large fishes' bodies, removing external parasites and dead scales.

The relationship between cleaner fishes and their host fishes has created an opportunity for a more dishonest fish. It is a false scavenger known in Latin as *Aspidontus taeniatus*. It is similar in size, form, color, and even in the way it performs an introductory "dance," to the cleaner fishes. In this way, it takes advantage of the host fishes' good faith. However it is not at all interested in doing any cleaning. When a host fish accepts the approach of this false cleaner, it receives only damaging bites in return.

POISONOUS LIFE IN THE REEF

Sea Scorpions

Like all other parts of the natural world, the reef has not only its beauties, but its dangers as well. These include the aforementioned false cleaners, the many vicious carnivores, and a modest collection of poisonous fishes. The last group is divided into two categories—those fishes that send out clear warning signals before attacking, and those

the ocean bottom, they remain motionless. This makes them almost invisible. And if they are touched, they extend their dorsal spines and strike.

Almost as poisonous as rockfish are the scorpaenids of the genus *Pterois* (lionfishes). Unlike rockfish, however, members of this genus usually are brightly and beautifully colored. They possess red or orange stripes

however, some small fishes find shelter in s[ ] urchin colonies.

Sea snakes are reptiles that belong to t[ ] family Hydrophiidae. This group is relat[ ] to cobras, mostly in the sense that they bo[ ] possess small, fixed front fangs. Some s[ ] snakes are very colorful, and all are very p[ ] sonous. Almost all sea snakes (except o[ ] species) are **viviparous**, meaning they gi[ ]

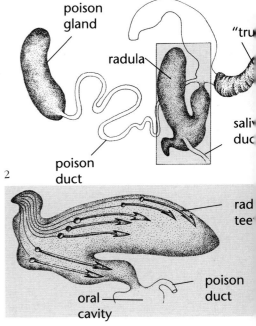

that don't. The second group prefers to rely on their own **camouflage** to ensure safety. Camouflage is a protective coloring that allows an animal to blend in with, and therefore seemingly "disappear" into, its surroundings.

Scorpaenids make up a family of poisonous fishes (Scorpaenidae). They are bottom-dwellers and carnivores. They have spines that protrude from the skeletal rays of their dorsal (back) fins. The most dangerous scorpaenids are the stonefishes (considered by some to make up their own family, Synanceiidae). They are a camouflage species that bear a striking resemblance to rocks. Their dorsal spines carry a deadly poison strong enough to kill a human within hours. In less serious cases, the poison causes gangrene (a severe epidermal infection that leads to the localized death and eventual sloughing of skin tissue).

The danger of rockfishes is of course magnified by their protective coloring. While on

and large ventral (belly) fins. Despite their dangerous qualities, they are popular aquarium subjects.

Poisoners Beyond Suspicion

A communication strategy of bright colors as signals has been adopted by the mollusks of the genus *Conus*. Like other gastropods, members of this genus possess a **radula**—a feeding organ with **chitinous** teeth. In their case, the radula makes and injects a strong poison that is used to capture the small prey. When necessary it also can be used against a careless shell gatherer that is not aware of the difference between cone shells and cyprea shells. The polychaetous annelids of the genus *Eurythoe* also are surprisingly poisonous.

Sea Urchins and Sea Snakes

Although not poisonous, sea urchins of the genus *Diadem* can inflict superifical wounds by using their long spines. Regardless of this,

birth to live young instead of laying eg[ ] Because of this, they do not have to leave t[ ] water in order to complete their reprodu[ ] tive cycle.

The Hydrophiidae is widely distributed[ ] the tropical waters of the Indian and Paci[ ] oceans. Fortunately for the people who l[ ] in those areas, they aren't aggressive cre[ ] tures. One member of the family, the beak[ ] sea snake (*Enhydrina schistosa*), reaches[ ] length of around 160 centimeters (62 in) a[ ] possesses the most potent venom of a[ ] snake in the world. However, again, it is[ ] gentle and passive creature, so bites are ve[ ] rare.

Among the many poisonous creatures of the tropical seas are fishes, sea urchins, sea stars, and sea cucumbers. One of the most unexpected and dangerous is the **1.** gastropod *Conus textile,* with its beautiful multicolored shell. It captures small animals such as fish, shrimp, and worms with poison darts it keeps in its **2.** radula. A radula is the feeding organ of mollusks. Darts are replaced as they

get used. The darts, "fired" by a retractile "trunk," are modified teeth. Fish-eating mollusks are very poisonous and potentially deadly, even to humans. Among poisonous fishes, the most noteworthy are **5.** stonefish (*Synanceia verrucosa*). They blend in with the ocean floor. Several varieties of brightly colored scorpionfish, of which the best known are **3.** *Pterois volitans* and **4.** *Pteropterus radiata*.

4

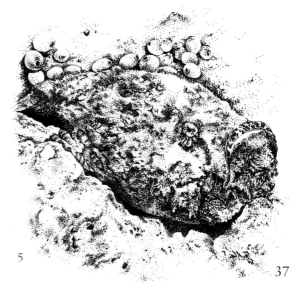

SHARKS

Swimmers for Survival

Low tide in an atoll drives all the fish into deeper water. The return of high tide brings not only the return of the water but also the larger inhabitants of the rocky underwater forest.

The first to return are the blackfin sharks (*Carcharodon melanopterus*). Blackfin sharks are specialized selachians that grow to about 1.5 meters (5 ft) in length. Thanks to their fairly flat shape, they can survive in water as shallow as 15 to 30 centimeters (6 to 12 in) and therefore never need to go into very deep water.

The relationship between these sharks and the island dwellers of the Australian

Predators for All Occasions

The anatomical traits of sharks are primitive when compared to those of bony fishes. However, as primitive as they may be, sharks still manage to fill many ecological niches.

Sharks are made up of a group of creatures that are both very similar and very different from one another. There are sharks of small and medium size that pose no danger to humans at all, then there are terrifying sharks such as the great white shark (*Carcharodon carcharias*), which has been known to cause many human deaths. This shark may grow as long as 12 meters (40 ft).

There are many harmless large sharks as

1

Great Barrier Reef could almost be called "friendly." Before attacking a swimmer who has come too close, the shark arches its back. This movement signals an unwillingness to take any aggressive action, giving the swimmer a chance to back off.

The blackfin shark does not have a **swim bladder**, which allows other fishes to float effortlessly in the water. Blackfin sharks also lack the muscles required to move water through their gills. Thus, they must swim constantly to keep from sinking or suffocating.

On a similar note, sharks that become trapped in any way die quickly. Anti-shark nets are used to protect swimmers off the coast of Queensland, Australia. These nets have caused the death of more than 20,000 sharks over the past 15 years or so. They have also caused the deaths of over 2600 sea turtles and more than 470 sea cows (also called "manatees"). Both of these animal groups are endangered.

well. Among them are the elephant shark (*Cetorhinus maximus*) and the whale shark (*Rhincodon typus*). These two species are the largest of all fishes. They may grow as long as

1. The white shark (*Carcharodon carcharias*). This marauder of the seas is able to tear a human to pieces.
2. Shark of the *Carcharodon* species, Bahamas. These sharks, easily identified by their tapered profile, are frequent visitors to the reef. They venture into water only 10 to 15 meters (33 to 50 ft) deep, as do the blackfin sharks (*C. melanopterus*) and the blacktail sharks (*C. wheeleri*). The latter sharks, however, flee at the sight of people. They may take to water as deep as 100 meters (330 ft). Another deep-water shark is the tiger shark (*Galeocerdo cuvier*). It is a real danger to people. It also feeds on fish, turtles, birds, and smaller sharks.

2

15 meters (50 ft) and 18 meters (60 ft), respectively. Both, however, feed only on plankton, thus neither is predatory toward humans.

Some sharks have unusual body designs. Examples of such sharks include the hammerhead shark (*Sphyrna zygaena*) and the sawfish (*Pristis zisjron*). The sawfish uses its long, sawlike appendage to stir up the ocean bottom in search of prey. The hammerhead shark has cylindrical appendages that extend horizontally from its snout. On each one is an eye and a nostril. Despite this bizarre, almost "science-fictionesque" appearance, this shark otherwise functions in traditional shark fashion. Given its size–4 meters (13.5 ft) in length and weighing an average of 675 kilograms (1,485 lbs)–the hammerhead can be a danger to people. This was proven in 1815 when human remains were found in the stomach of a hammerhead caught off the coast of Long Island, New York.

Sharks depend mostly on their sense of smell and something called their "lateral line" to locate prey. The lateral line is a sense organ that starts behind the eye and runs to the base of the tail. It is made up of a series of long, branching canals filled with hair-like cells that are located under the skin. The lateral line can pick up changes in water movement caused by other creatures. It can also give clues as to the position as well as the size and speed of the creature causing the movement.

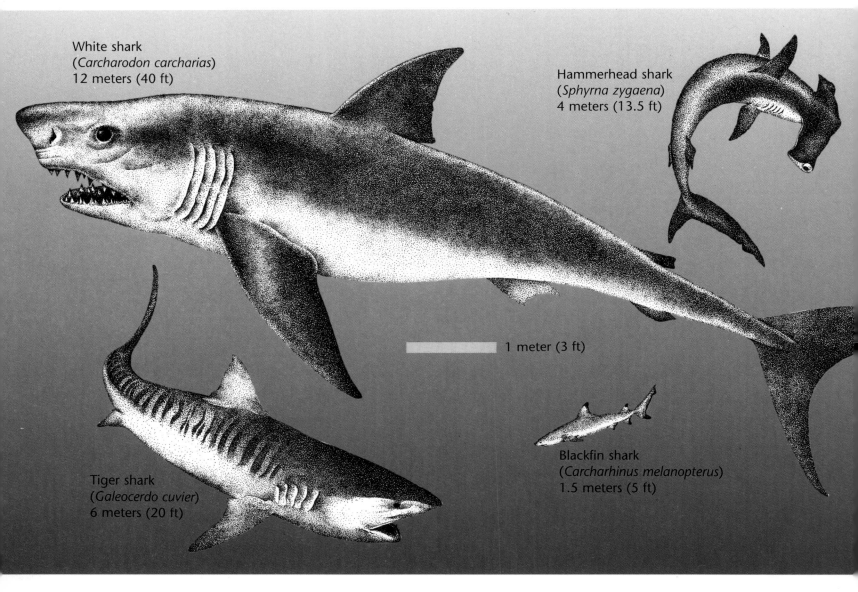

White shark
(*Carcharodon carcharias*)
12 meters (40 ft)

Hammerhead shark
(*Sphyrna zygaena*)
4 meters (13.5 ft)

1 meter (3 ft)

Blackfin shark
(*Carcharhinus melanopterus*)
1.5 meters (5 ft)

Tiger shark
(*Galeocerdo cuvier*)
6 meters (20 ft)

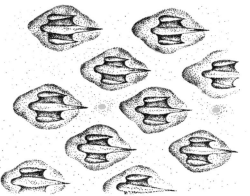

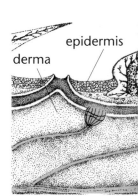

epidermis

derma

2

3   4

1. Sharks belong to an order of Selachians. There are fewer shark species than ray species (250 species of the former, 350 of the latter). Sharks, however, are more distinct and varied than rays. Among the species illustrated is the sawfish. It belongs to a specialized family of rays, as is shown by the position of the gills below the pectoral fins. Small sawfish (family Pristidae) (1 to 2 meters/3 to 6 ft) do exist.

2. Sharks have a sensory organ—the lateral line—on either side of their body. This organ sends to the brain sound waves that vibrate through the water. Sharks use their ears only to keep their balance. When hunting, a shark follows a spiral path. The waves made by prey moving in the water are sensed more on the right side of the shark if the prey is to the shark's right.

3. Diagram of shark skin, greatly enlarged. The skin is rough to the touch because it contains many hard scales. Each is made up of a dentine base and a sharp point covered with enamel. The scales point toward the fish's tail.
4. A longitudinal section of shark skin. The lateral line appears in yellow.

Gray reef shark
(*Carcharhinus amblyrhynchos*)
1.5 meters (5 ft)

Whale shark
(*Rhincodon typus*)
18 meters (60 ft)

Nurse shark
(*Nebrius ferrugineus*)
4.2 meters (14.5 ft)

Sawfish
(*Pristis zisjron*)
4.5 meters (15 ft)

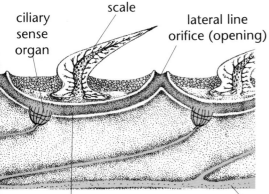

ciliary
sense
organ

scale

lateral line
orifice (opening)

lateral line canal

Branch of the tenth encephalic nerve

THE FUTURE OF THE REEF

Coral Reef and Tropical Forest

The coral reef is one of the Earth's most fascinating marine environments, while the most fascinating land environment probably is the tropical rain forest. For this reason, the two ecosystems are often compared. Both contribute much to the splendor and biological richness of our planet.

Coral reefs cover a total area of 600,000 square kilometers (more than 230,000 square mi). This is equal to about 0.2 percent of Earth's entire water surface. In total area, the coral reefs are much smaller than the rain forests, which cover about 7.5 mil-

organisms move back onto the rocks and continue on with life as usual. Among these are many coral larvae, which quickly begin to compete for space. As you might imagine, competition for reef space is fierce. About 200 larvae colonies initially settle on a square meter (3.45 square ft) of bare rock. However, only three or four will still be there a few years later. Some corals can send out filaments that digest adjacent colonies. This whole competition process continues until a new disaster wipes them out again.

The aforementioned second destructive force, the sea star (*Acanthaster planci*), is

In many areas of the coral reef, **1.** people gather beautiful mollusk shells for sale as souvenirs. This is the fate of the gastropod **2.** *Charonia tritonis*, or giant triton, which has become rare. The triton is the main predator of the **3.** large sea star *Acanthaster planci*, or "crown of thorns." This sea star feeds on coral madrepores. The madrepores are sucked from their thecas, leaving

lion square kilometers (2.9 million square mi) of the Earth. This is equal to about 6 percent of the Earth's total land surface.

Considering their limited size, the coral reefs seem to hold a greater biological wealth than the rain forests. It has been calculated that about one-third of all fish species are found in coral reefs. It is also very possible that many small species remain undiscovered.

Reef Destroyers

The entities that most drastically alter reefs are, believe it or not, 1) hurricanes, and 2) a sea star that has between 11 and 22 arms.

Hurricanes can quickly and effortlessly sweep away vast stretches of reef. However, within a few hours of their passing, many

also known as the crown of thorns. A single crown of thorns can digest 6 square meters (21 square ft) of coral in one year. Think of the mass destruction it can cause when it begins to multiply excessively.

Some episodes of sudden growth in the number of crowns of thorns have been directly linked to human activity. In particular, the fishing of some animals that prey on the crown of thorns obviously has been a problem. These predators include several fishes and at least one mollusk—the giant triton (*Charonia tritonis*). On the other hand, attacks by crowns of thorns play a key role in regulating the overgrowth of some coral species, which in turn provides colonization opportunities for "weaker" species.

behind a stretch of whitening skeletons. In the absence of tritons, the number of *Acanthaster* can multiply to the point where whole parts of a reef are destroyed.

ENVIRONMENT: crown-of-thorns
starfish feeds and kills coral colony

RAS MOHAMED (EGYPT)
THE EGYPTIAN NATIONAL RESERVE

LES TORTUES À BALI
INDONESIE

he Maldive Islands, some beach
have hired divers equipped with
and knives to gather up excessive
of thorns and leave them on the
dry. In 1990, in the Nakatchafushi
more than 18,000 specimens were
d in this way.

ever, this approach offers only short-
lief to an environment that is also
by pollutants. Most corals are high-
tive to simple tidal movements and
sensitive to the blanketing effects of
ts. Blanket pollutants such as mud,
a fine white mineral clay), and land-

fill are especially harmful to reefs.

For the past several years, destruction of
the tropical rain forest has also had a nega-
tive effect on reefs. Tropical rains erode land
that is not held in place by protective vegetation. This erosion increases with the opening of coastal roads. Often these roads are
covered with sand and coralline debris, both
of which are easily washed into the sea.

On the island of Guam, a road that
opened along the southern coast caused the
extinction of 95 percent of the coral. A similar event occurred in Queensland, Australia.
Here, debris from highway construction at

the edge of the rain forest at Daint
caused severe damage to the local ree

Similar situations result from d
the sea bottom to build or enlarge
Such damage also occurs during the
of coralline rock. In the atolls of the
and Indian oceans, the reefs offer rea
economical building material. In
years, however, the rate at which this
ial has been mined has exceeded the s
which the polyps can renew it. This
has also led to a sharp decrease in lo
populations.

Kodachrome
FILM

Causes of Pollution

lly the waters around coral reefs are
nd clear, and their nutrient content is
r this reason, reefs are very sensitive
-made pollutants.

the island of Oahu, Hawaii, agricul-
and urban development around
ilu Bay has caused great changes in
f community. In the early 1970s, the
began to cloud, the algae and the
s grew out of control, and the
ores began to die.

i in 1978, the sewage discharge ducts
ere causing many of these problems

1. An Indonesian rinses the remains of
a marine turtle before removing its shell.
Shells are made into pins, boxes, fans,
combs, and other objects. The meat ends
up on a gourmet's table or in a restaurant.
Hunting is one cause of the decline of
marine reptiles living near coral reefs. To
protect the animals without harming the
economies of developing nations, some
Caribbean islands captive-raise sea turtles.
This involves harvesting the eggs from the
holes where they have been buried in the
sand (a place where baby sea turtles
emerging from their shells are subject

to being eaten by marine birds), ar
incubation, the raising of young tur
and the release of older turtles into
sea. In this way, some turtles that w
have been lost to natural predators
be sacrificed for commercial uses w
endangering the species in nature.
2. An oil-drilling platform. Oil pollu
of the ocean is a serious problem. T
problem does not only affect coral

Explosion of the first hydrogen bomb at Eniwetok Atoll in the South Pacific on October 31, 1952.

xtended to the open sea. Within a few
he status of the sponges, algae, and
ores began to improve. The sponges
algae decreased, and the madrepores
o reappear. However, since 1990, the
ave begun to grow again. This may be
the development of local areas.
ng the sources of pollution that
arine life (solvents, dyes, heavy met-
), two are especially threatening—oil
ioactive wastes. Transportation acci-
ause some oil pollution, but the
methods used to find and produce
il offshore offer much greater risks.

Chemical lubricants used in drilling are very toxic to marine organisms, as are chemical agents used to clean up oil spills.

Radioactive pollutants have also resulted from the testing of nuclear warheads. This testing involved, and still involves, Pacific atolls occupied by the United States, France, and Great Britain. These atolls include Bikini, Eniwetok, Johnston, Kiritimati, Fangataufa, and Mururoa. These names have come to have deep meaning for those engaged in struggles that favor the environment. At these sites, nuclear experiments have been carried out in the air, under-

ground, and underwater. Each exp
has had harmful effects on the natur
and fauna. Some radioactive resic
accumulated in the sea, and this resi
serious threat to the future of these
plus others.

PAPEETE,TAHITI,9/2/95 DEMONSTRATION
US NUCLEAR TESTING

1. Explosion of the first H-bomb duri
series of nuclear experiments in the S
Pacific. The experiments began in the
1950s. This is Eniwetok Atoll, Octobe
1952.
2. On September 2, 1995 in Papeete
Tahiti, on another Pacific atoll, people
protest against nuclear testing.

TROPICAL RAIN FOREST

7.5 million square kilometers (2.9 million square mi)

6 percent of the total land area

50 percent of all living species

There is a relationship between the size of an area and the number of plant and animal species it can support. This relationship holds true only when comparing similar environments. On our planet there are environments in which, thanks to the large variety and richness of available ecological niches, an unusually high number of species exist. This is most obvious in the tropical rain forests. While

100 percent of all species living on land

CORAL REEFS
600,000 square kilometers (230,000 square mi)

0.2 percent of total ocean surface

33 percent of existing marine species

covering only 6 percent of Earth's surface area, tropical rain forests host about 50 percent of all Earth's species. In the sea, the coral reef is a more extreme example. In an area of only about 600,000 square kilometers (230,000 square mi), or 0.2 percent of the ocean surface, coral reefs are home to about 33 percent of the species that live in Earth's water.

100 percent of the species living in all the oceans

GLOSSARY

Words in *italics* can be found elsewhere in the glossary.

Actiniae Order of *Anthozoa* that are fairly large in size, lack a *calcareous* skeleton, are solitary, have many tentacles, and live as *polyps*. Sea anemones belong in this group. A member of this order is referred to as an "actiniid."

annelids Group of worms that have segmented bodies.

Anthozoa Class of solitary or colonial *cnidarians* that live as *polyps* and have circular mouths with a crown of tentacles that are used for feeding.

asexual reproduction Creation of new individuals from a single parent. The offspring are genetically identical to the parent.

atoll Ring-shaped reef made up of *calcareous* algae and *madrepores* that encloses a *lagoon* and is surrounded by open sea.

bivalve Mollusk characterized as having a two-part shell.

Bryozoa Class of colonial marine invertebrates that are sometimes called "moss animals."

calcareous Made of calcium carbonate ($CaCO_3$), which is also known as limestone.

camouflage Coloration and patterning of an organism that allows it to blend in with its surroundings.

cay Flat, sandy, or coralline island dotted with vegetation.

Ceriantharia Order of solitary *Anthozoa* that live in small tubes they build themselves.

chitinous Made of chitin, the main substance of the cuticle (tough outer layer) and exoskeletons of some worms, insects, and crustaceans.

cilia (sing. cilium) Short, hairlike structures that grow from a cell and are used by some organisms for hunting or movement.

cnidaria Phylum of animals that have cup-shaped bodies and tentacles that contain stinging cells called *nematocysts*.

colony Group of organisms, often of the same species, that live together, depend on each other, and sometimes function as a single unit.

coralline island Land structure made up of coral that is completely surrounded by water.

ctenophores Group of invertebrate marine carnivores that are closely related to the *cnidarians*. They have translucent, rainbow-colored bodies that are propelled by eight bands of moving hair-like *cilia*.

ecosystem The community of organisms and the non-living factors of the environment that occupy a specific area.

foot In mollusks, a muscular organ that is used for movement or to attach to or penetrate a solid base.

gastropod Mollusk having a well-developed head with tentacles, a large flattened foot, and often a coiled and twisted shell.

gastrovascular cavity Body section that carries out digestion and circulation.

hermaphrodite An organism that has functioning male and female reproductive organs.

hermatype coral *Anthozoa* known as "hard" or "rocky" coral. They contain *zooxanthellae*. Their *calcareous* skeletons make them the most important group of reef builders.

Hydrozoa Class of solitary or colonial *cnidarians* that can live as polyps or medusas; the group includes both freshwater and saltwater hydras.

inner slope Incline descending from the *reef flat* that forms the external *lagoon* of an *atoll*.

knoll Submerged *madrepore* pinnacle, situated between the inner and outer *lagoons* of an *atoll*.

lagoon Shallow basin of water that is separated from the open sea by a *coral reef* but connected to it by a *tidal channel*.

lateral line An external sense organ in shark that detects vibrations and changes in water movement.

life cycle The process of changes that an organism passes through from birth to death.

limestone A sedimentary rock made up mostly of carbonate minerals such as calcium or magnesium.

madrepore islet Formation of a *reef flat* that emerges from the water.

madrepores The reef-building coral group; they have a *calcareous* skeleton in the form of a cup-like *theca*.

mantle In *mollusks*, the organ that produces and lines the inside of the shell and extends beyond its edges; an extension of the digestive sac that is the soft body of a *mollusk*.

marl A type of rock that is crumbly, like clay.

medusa The solitary, sexually reproducing and free-floating plankton form of many *cnidarians*. Medusas have an umbrella-shaped body made mostly of water, a mouth that faces downward, ringed with tentacles and a body surface dotted with *nematocysts*.

mimicry The quality of resembling another organism, usually for the purpose of casting the impression of being dangerous (because the organism that is being "copied" is genuinely dangerous).

moat Area of a coral reef that is immediately adjacent to the internal side of the ridge which protects the moat from waves while still allowing the circulation of well-oxygenated water from the open sea.

mollusks Group of terrestrial and aquatic invertebrates that have a *mantle*, a *foot*, and sometimes *shells*—external (oysters and nautiluses) or internal (cuttlefish).

nematocyst Stinging cell of a *cnidarian*.

phylum (plural **phyla**) Group of organisms smaller than a kingdom (which is the largest classification group in the taxonomic system, i.e., the "top" group).

plankton Tiny marine organisms that float freely in water; they serve as food for marine animals that filter feed.

polychaeta Class of marine invertebrates belonging to the annelids; its features are a worm-like appearance with a body made up of successive longitudinal segments, many bristly tufts, and an elegant gill plume.

polyps *Cnidarians* that live attached to a surface and have a tube-like body topped by a mouth fringed with one or more tentacles that reach upward.

radula Feeding organ in the mouths of *mollusks* made up of a continually renewed chitinous ribbon armed with rows of primitive teeth that serve to scrape food from surfaces and grind it before ingestion.

reef In oceanography, a massive formation of calcareous rock that reaches just above or below the surface of the water and is built up from the ocean floor by the accumulation of skeletons of animals and algae.

reef flat Level part of an *atoll*, at most just barely submerged.

ridge Outer part of the *coral reef* that, although still covered by the sea, is 36 centimeters (14 in) or higher than the section immediately adjacent to the inside of the reef.

Scyphozoa Class of *cnidarians* that live as *medusas* and include the jellyfishes.

sea star Spiny animal (echinoderm) that has a body made up of a central disk surrounded by tapering rays or arms. Sea stars are often called "starfish."

selachian Cartilaginous fish, such as sharks, rays, and related species.

serranid Any of the carnivorous fishes of the family Serranidae, including groupers and sea bass.

sexual reproduction Creation of new individuals through the union of two gametes (male and female reproductive cells), each of which brings a copy of only one gene for each trait from the pair in each parent's gene pool.

shell Protective *calcareous* covering produced by the *mantle* of certain *mollusks*.

subsidence Process by which a delta or other land area sinks under water.

swim bladder Organ of a fish that allows the animal to change or maintain its depth in the water.

symbiosis Relationship between two organisms in which each benefits from the characteristics and activities of the other.

theca Cup-like structure that, along with thin dividing laminae (scales), makes up the *calcareous* skeleton of the *madrepores*.

tidal channel Natural canal that connects a *lagoon* within a *coral reef* to the open sea.

viviparous To give birth to living young rather than laying eggs.

zooxanthellae Single-celled, microscopic, photosynthetic algae that live in *symbiosis* with *madrepores*, some *mollusks*, and some sponges.

FURTHER READING

Baines, John D. *Protecting the Oceans.* (Conserving Our World Series). Raintree Steck-Vaughn, 1990

Bramwell, Martyn. *The Oceans* (revised edition). Watts, 1994

Conway, Lorraine. *Oceanography.* Good Apple, 1982

Editors, Raintree Steck-Vaughn. *The Raintree Steck-Vaughn Illustrated Science Encyclopedia* (1997 edition). (24 volumes). Raintree Steck-Vaughn, 1997

Fodor, R. V. *The Strange World of Deep-Sea Vents.* (Earth Processes Series). Enslow Publishers, 1991

George, Michael. *Coral Reef.* (Images Series). Creative Education, 1992

Gutnik, Martin J. and Browne-Gutnik, Natalie. *Great Barrier Reef.* (Wonders of the World Series). Raintree Steck-Vaughn, 1994

Holig, Dwight, et al. *Coral Reefs.* (Close Up: A Focus on Nature Series). Silver Burdett Press, 1994

Johnson, Rebecca L. *The Great Barrier Reef: A Living Laboratory.* (Discovery! Series). Lerner Group, 1991

Lambert, David. *The Pacific Ocean.* (Seas and Oceans Series). Raintree Steck-Vaughn, 1996

Lambert, David and McConnell, Anita. *Seas and Oceans.* (World of Science Series). Facts on File, 1985

Markle, Sandra. *Pioneering Ocean Depths.* Simon and Schuster, 1994

Mattson, Robert A. *The Living Ocean.* (Living World Series). Enslow Publishers, 1991

Morgan, Nina. *The Caribbean and the Gulf of Mexico.* (Seas and Oceans Series). Raintree Steck-Vaughn, 1996

————. *The North Sea and the Baltic Sea.* (Seas and Oceans Series). Raintree Steck-Vaughn, 1996

Naden, Corinne J. and Blue, Rose. *The Black Sea.* (Wonders of the World Series). Raintree Steck-Vaughn, 1995

Neal, Philip. *The Oceans.* (Conservation 2000 Series). Trafalgar, 1993

Pifer, Joanne. *EarthWise: Earth's Oceans.* (EarthWise Series). WP Press, 1992

Sargent, William. *Night Reef: Dusk to Dawn on a Coral Reef.* (New England Aquarium Books). Watts, 1991

Tesar, Jenny. *Threatened Oceans.* (Our Fragile Planet Series). Facts on File, 1992

Waterlow, Julia. *The Atlantic Ocean.* (Seas and Oceans Series). Raintree Steck-Vaughn, 1996

INDEX

Note: page numbers in *italics* indicate illustrations

budefduf sp., *28-29*
canthaster planci, 42, *43*
canthurus lineatus, 30
cropora, 26
cropora sp. madrepore, *23*
ctiniae, 17
  as order, 16
ctiniids, 16
daptation(s):
  blackfin shark, 38
  clownfish, 34
  color as, 28-32, *32*
  fish, 32
  long, narrow snouts, 32, *33*
  reef creatures, 26
  sharks', 40
lcyonarian coral (*Sarophyton*), 27
lgae:
  habitat of, 26
  symbiotic relationship of, with giant
    clam, 26
lps, calcareous, *12*
mphiprion, 34
mphiprion bincinctus, *35*
ngelfish family, 30
  and color as identification, *28*
ntennae, *34*
nthozoa:
  as group, 16, *17*
  madrepores as, 16
nthozoan cnidarians, as required for
  coral reef, 12
nti-shark nets, 38
quatic environment:
  appreciation/respect for, 9
  as dumping ground, 9
  See also Ocean(s); Sea(s)
rmored boxfish, poisons of, 32
rtificial incubation, 45
sbestos, 9
sexual reproduction, defined, 18
spidontus taeniatus, 34
tlantic Ocean, lack of reefs in, 28
tolls, *12-13*
  defined, 13
  Great Australian Barrier Reef, 22
  nuclear testing on, 46-47
ulostomus maculatus, 32
ustralia
  coral reefs in, 12, *13*
  Great Barrier Reef of, *14-15*
ustralian Barrier Reef pools, 22-27, *23,
  24, 25, 26*

Balistapus undulatus, 30
Banded clownfish (*Heractis magnifica*), *35*
Barrier reefs, location of true, *13*
Beaked sea snake (*Enhydrina
    schistosa*), 36
Bigeye (*Priacanthus hamrur*), *31*
Bikini atoll, 46
Bivalves, 23
"Black coral," *14*
Blackfin shark (*Carcharodon
    melanopterus*), 38, *39, 40*
Blacktail shark (*C. wheeleri*), 39
Blanket pollutants, 44
Blennoids, 29
Bodianus anthioides, *31*
Body designs, sharks', 40-41
Boulder coral (*Montastrea cabernosa*),
    14, *19, 21*
Brain coral, *17, 21*
Bromine, 9
Bush corals, *35*
Butterfly fish, and use of color, 29

Caesia suevicus, *2-3*
Calcareous, defined, 13
Calcium bicarbonate (Ca[HCO$_3$]$_2$), 18
  recycling of, 13
Calcium carbonate (CaCO$_3$), 18
Calcium carbonate skeleton,
    madrepore's, 16
Camouflage, defined, 36
Carbon dioxide (CO$_2$), 18
Carcharhinus amblyrhynchos, *41*
Carcharodon carcharias, 38, *39, 40*
Carcharodon melanopterus, 38, *39, 40*
Caribbean Sea:
  coral in, *21*
  madrepore species in, 18
Cardinalfish (*Siphamia versicolor*), 34
Caripidae family, 32
Carnivores, 36
Cays, features of, 23
Centropyge flavissimus, 30
Cephalopholis aurantius, 32
Cephalopholis miniata, 32
Cerianthus viridis, *17*
Cetorhinus maximus, 38-40
Chaetodon semilarvatus, *2-3*
Chaetodontidae (chaetodontids), 29, 32
Charonia tritonis, 42
Chemicals, value of, 9
Chitinous teeth, *36*
Christmas Island angelfish (*Centropyge
    flavissimus*), 30
Cilia, described, 16
Ciphoma gibbosum, *35*

Clams, as home for pearlfish, 32
Cleaner shrimp (*Periclimenes pedersoni*), *34*
Cleaning stations, 34
Clownfish, and sea anemones, 34, *35*
Cnidarian(s), described, 16, *17*
Coastal reefs, location of, *12*
Cobras, 36
Colonies, madrepores, 16
  layering of, *12*
  thecas in, 16
Color(s):
  as communication strategy, 36
  function of, 28
  as identification, *28*
  lionfish, 36
  as protection, 36, *37*
Cone shells, vs. cyprea shells, 36
Conus textile, 36
Coral, 12
  in Great Barrier Reef, *23, 27*
  See also Madrepores
Coral atoll, 12
  See also Atoll
Coral isle, *15*
Coral larvae, competition of, 42
Coralline island, formation of, 18
Coralline rock, *14*
Coral reef(s):
  area of, 42
  biological wealth of, 42
  birth of, *10-11*, 10-15
  as building material, 44
  effect of destruction of tropical rain
    forest on, 44
  existing marine species in, *49*
  as fish paradise, 28
  global arrangements of, *12-13*
  hiding places in, 29, 32, *33*
  as land environment, 42
  model of, *14-15*
  ocean surface area of, *49*
  as paradise for people, 28
  physical elements required for, *12-13*
  species in, *49*
  as tropical marine ecosystem, *16-21*
Crannies, in coral reef, 32, *33*
"Crown of thorns," 42, *43*
  harvesting of, 44
Crystalloid sacs, function of, *24-25*
Ctenophores, 16, *17*
Cyprea (*Ovula ovum*) gastropods, 26
  shells of, 36

"Dance," and symbiotic relationship, 34
Dappled grouper (*Epinephelus tauvina*), *34*
Darts, *36*

Darwin, Charles, on phases of coral formation, 12
Deep sea madrepore, *14*
Design, purpose of fishes', 32
See also Body designs
Diadem genus, 32, 36
Diet:
elephant shark, 40
giant clam, 24
of plankton, 18
polyps, 16
sea star, 42
tiger shark, *39*
triggerfish, 32
whale shark, 40
Diodon hystrix, *31*
Diodontidae family, 32
Diploria labyrinthiformis, *21*
Dolomite Alps, formation of, *12*
Double-banded clownfish (*Amphiprion bincinctus*), 35
Dredging, effect of, on coral reefs, 44
Dyes, as sources of pollution, 46

Ears, sharks' use of, *41*
Eibl-Eibesfeldt, Irenaus, 34
Elactinus oceanops, as "cleaners," 34
Elephant shark (*Cetorhinus maximus*), 38-40
Elkhorn coral, *17*
Emperor angelfish (*Pomacanthus imperator*), *32*
Endangered species, 38
Enhydrina schistosa, 36
Eniwetok atoll, H-bomb explosion on, 46
Epinephelus flavocoeruleus, description of, 29
Epinephelus spp., 34
Epinephelus tauvina, 34
Erosion:
on coastal roads, 44
in Dolomites, 13
and tropical rains, 44
Ethologist, defined, 34
Eurythoe genus, 36

False cleaners, 34, 36
False scavengers, 34
Fan corals, *35*
Fangataufa atoll, 46
Fins:
dorsal, 36
pectoral, 41
ventral, 36
Fish(es), *28-33, 29, 30, 31, 32*
adaptations of, 32
colors of, 28-29
habitat of, 28
poisonous, 36-37

protective features of, 32
varieties of, 29-32
Fissures, in coral reef, *33*
Flamingo-tongue (*Ciphoma gibbosum*), *35*
Food, gathering in reefs, *32, 33*
See also Diet
Foxfish (*Lo vulpinus*), *32*
France, nuclear testing of, 46-47
French angelfish (*Pomacanthus paru*), 28-29, *30*
Fringing reefs, location of, 12

Gangrene, defined, 36
Gastropod (*Charonia tritonis*), 42
Gastropod (*Conus textile*), 36
Gastropod mollusks, 18
Gastrovascular cavity, madrepores, 16
Giant clam:
life of, 23-26, *24, 25*
symbiotic relationship of, 24
Giant triton (*Charonia tritonis*), 42
Gills:
crowns of, 23
sawfish, *41*
Glucose, 18
Gnathypops rosenbergi, 32
Gobius ucchichii, 35
Goby (*Gobius ucchichii*), 35
Gorgonian(s), 15, 16, *28-29*
mantle of, *35*
Gorgonian coral, *33*
Grand Cayman Islands, Caribbean Sea, *35*
Gray reef shark (*Carcharhinus amblyrhynchos*), *41*
Great Barrier Reef of Australia, *14-15*
fish species in, 28
madrepore species in, 18
size of, 23
Great Britain, nuclear testing of, 46-47
Great white shark (*Carcharodon carcharias*), 38, *39, 40*
Green Island, *14-15*
Grotto, *14*
Groupers, symbiotic relationships of, 34
Guam, effect of building a road on, 44
Gullies, as refuge, 18

Habitat(s):
algae, 26
baby sea turtles, 45
fish, 28
madrepores, 18
pearlfish, 32
scorpaenids, 36
sea snakes, 36
sharks, 38, *39*
Hammerhead sharks (*Sphyrna zygaena*):
body design of, *40*

danger of, 40
Hawkfish (*Oxycirrhitus typus*), 33
H-bomb, explosion of, *46*
Heavy metals, as sources of pollution, 4⟨
Heractis magnifica, *35*
Herbivores, 29
Hermaphrodites, reproduction in, 33
Heteractic magnifica, *17*
Hexacoral, *16-17*
Holy water fonts, giant clam shells as, 2⟨
Honolulu Bay, pollution of, 45
Hormiphora plumosa, *17*
Hunting:
marine reptiles, *44, 45*
method of sharks', *41*
Hurghada, Egypt, coral reef at, *2-3*
Hurricanes, danger of, 42
Hydras, 16
Hydrophiidae family, 36
Hydrozoa, 16, *17*

Indian Ocean:
reefs of, 28-29, 44
sea snakes in, 36
Industry, and damage to aquatic environment, 9
Inner cavity, cnidarian's, 16

Jaws, function of fishes', 32
Jellyfish(es), 16
Johnston atoll, 46

Kaolin, as pollutant, 44
Kiritimati atoll, 46
Klunzinger's wrasse (*Thalassoma klunzingen*), *31*

Labroides dimidiatus, as "cleaner," 34
Lagoons, *15*
Lambis lambis, 26
Land environment, coral reef as, 42
Landfill, as pollutant, 44
Larvae, 18
Lateral line, sharks', *40-41*
Lead, 9
Length (of):
blackfin shark, 38, *40*
elephant shark, 40
giant clam, 24-25
gray reef shark, *41*
great white shark, *38, 40*
hammerhead shark, *40*
nurse shark, *41*
sawfish, *40*
sea snake, 36
serranid, 29
tiger shark, *40*
whale shark, 40, *41*
white shark, 40

enses, giant clam's, 24-26
ettuce-leaf coral, *17*
ettuce-leaf madrepore colony
   (*Montispora* sp.), *14, 20*
ife cycle(s), madrepores', 12-13
ight:
   from crystalline sacs, *24-25*
   dependence on, 26
mestone, 13, 16
inckia laevigata, 27
onfish (*Pterois*), 36
ps, giant clam, 24-25
ithophytum arboreum, 16
ong-nosed triggerfish (*Oxymonacanthus*
   longerostris), 31
o vulpinus, 32
utjanidae family, 29
yretail (Bodianus anthioides), 31

Madrepore(s), *16-17*
   brain-shaped, *23*
   growth of, 18
   as hexacorals, *18-19*
   as required for coral reefs, 12
   as sea star victim, 42-43, *43*
adrepore colonies, habitat of, 18
aldive Islands, 44
anatee(s). *See* sea cows
antle:
   clam, 26
   mollusk vs. gorgonian, *35*
arine reptiles, decline of, 44, 45
arine turtles, 44, 45
arl, 13
asked butterfly fish (*Chaetodon*
   semilarvatus), 2-3
astigias sp., 17
edusa, defined, 16
ercury, 9
erlet's scorpionfish (*Rhinopias*
   aphanes), 30
inerals, value of, 9
oat, 15
ollusks, fish-eating, *37*
ucus, as protection, 34
ud, as pollutant, 44
ururoa atoll, 46
ushroom coral, *17*
utual aid societies, *34-35*

akatchafushi area, 44
ebrius ferrugineus, 41
ematocysts:
   described, 16
   function of, 16-18
uclear experiments, harmful effects of, 46
uclear warheads, testing of, 46-47
urse shark (*Nebrius ferrugineus*), 41
utrition, waters as source of, 9

Oahu, Hawaii, pollution in, 45-46
Ocean(s):
   damage to, 9
   value of, 9
Octocoral, *16-17*
Oil drilling, as source of pollution, 46
Oil-drilling platform, *45*
Oil pollution, 45
Ostraciidae family, 32
Osymonacanthus longirostris, 31
Ovula ovum, 26
Oxycirrhitus typus, 33

Pacific Ocean:
   reefs in, 28-29, 44
   sea snakes in, 36
Papeete, Tahiti, protests of nuclear
   testing, 47
Papua New Guinea, 21
Parazoanthus axinellae, 17
Parrotfish (*Scarus ferrugineus*), 18, 29, 30
   jaws of, 32
Patterns, function of, 28
Pearl(s), 9
Pearlfish, food/shelter for, 32
Pennatula rubra (sea feather), *17*
Periclimenes pedersoni, 34
Photosynthesis, and need for light, 18
Plankton, 18, 40
Plastics, 9
Platax pinnatus, 31
Plectorhinchus spp., 34
Plectropomus maculatus, description of,
   29-32
Plumularia pinnata, 17
Poison:
   and color, in fish, 32
   in reef life, 36-37
Poisonous fish(es), *36-37*
   categories of, 36
Pollutants, effect of, on coral, 44
Pollution:
   causes of, 45-46
   sources of, 46-47
Polychaetous annelids, 18
   Eurythoe genus, 36
   Spirobranchus gigantus, 27
Polychaetous worms, 23
Polyps, 12
   defined, 16
"Polypus," defined, 16
Pomacanthidae, 28
Pomacanthus paru, 28-29, 30
Pomacanthus xanthometopon, 30
Porcupinefish (*Diodon hystrix*), 31
   protective features of, 32
Predator(s):
   Acanthaster planci (crown of thorns),
   42, 43

fish as, 29
hawkfish, *33*
Lutjanidae family, 29
sea star as, 23, 42, *43*
sharks as, 40
Priacanthus hamrur, 29, 31
Protection:
   camouflage, 36
   color as, 29
   methods of, 32
   mucus as, 34
   porcupinefish, 32
   sea turtles, 44, 45
   swelling as, 32
   thorns as, 32
Pseudanthias dispar, 31
Pseudanthias squamipinnis, 19, 33
Pseudanthias tuka, 31
Pterois, 36
Pterois volitans, 37
Pteropterus radiata, 37
Puffers, protective features of, 32
Purple serranid (*Pseudanthias tuka*), 31

Queensland, Australia, *14-15*
   anti-shark nets, 38
   reef damage at, 44

Radioactive wastes, as sources of
   pollution, 46-47
Radula, 36
Ras Mohammed, Red Sea, 33
Rays, vs. sharks, *41*
Red algae, 18
Red coralline seaweed, 14
Red-finned serranid (*Pseudanthias*
   dispar), 31
Red Sea, 35
   coral reefs in, *2-3*, 12
   serranids in, 32
   sponges in, *28-29*
Reef(s):
   destruction of, 42-43
   future of, *42-49, 43, 44, 45, 46, 47, 48*
   outer slope of, *15*
   "remodeling" of, 18
   See also Coral
Reef-builders, tiny, *16-21, 17, 18, 19, 20*
Reef flat, *14, 15*
Reproduction:
   asexual, 18
   forms of, 18
   hermaphrodites, *33*
   sea snakes, 36
Rhincodon typus, 41
Rhinopias aphanes, 30
Ridge, *15*
Rockfish (*Synanceia verrucosa*), 36, 37

Salt, 9
Sarcophyton, 27
Sawfish (*Pristis zisjron*), 40, 41
Scales, shark, *40-41*
Scarus ferrugineus (parrotfish), *30*
Scorpaenidae, 36
Scorpionfish, *37*
Scyphozoa, 16, *17*
Sea(s):
    damage to, 9
    value of, 9
Sea anemones, 16, *17*
    symbiotic relationships of, 34, *35*
Seabat (*Platax pinnatus*), *31*
Sea cows, anti-shark nets and, 38
Sea cucumbers, 23
    as home for pearlfish, 32
    as poisonous, *37*
Sea feather, *17*
Sea scorpions, 36, *37*
Sea snakes, 36, *37*
Sea stars (*Acanthaster planci*) 27
    as home for pearlfish, 32
    as poisonous, *37*
    as predators, 23, 42, *43*
    See also Crown of thorns
Sea turtles:
    anti-shark nets and, 38
    captive-raised, 45
Sea urchins, 23
    and cardinalfish, 34
    dangers of, 36, *37*
    as home for pearlfish, 32
Sediments, function of, 13
Selachian order, *41*
Sense organs, shark's lateral line as, 40, *41*
Sergeantfish (*Abudefduf* sp.), *28-29*
Serranidae family (serranids), *31, 33*
    description of, 29-32
    habitat of, 32, *33*
Sessile stage, 16
Sewage, 9
    discharge ducts, 45-46
Sexual reproduction, 18
Seychelle Islands, school of fish in, 29
Shape:
    blackfin sharks, 38
    Carcharodon sharks, *39*
    See also Body designs
Sharks: *38-41, 39, 40*
    anatomical traits of, 38, *40-41*
    vs. rays, *41*
    sizes of, 38, *40-41*
Shark skin, *40-41*
Shells, 9
    Cyprea gastropods (*Ovula ovum*), 27
    as souvenirs, 42, 45

Shoals, as habitat for madrepores, 12
Shrimp (*Periclimenes pedersoni*), as cleaners, *34*
Siganidids, 32
Sipadan Island, Borneo, *20*
Siphamia versicolor (cardinalfish), 34
Size:
    and "cleaner" relationship, 34
    fish, 29
    polyps, 16
    shark, 38, 40
Skeleton, outer shape of madrepore's, 18
Smell, shark's sense of, 40
Snouts, long, narrow, 32, *33*
Solvents, as source of pollution, 46
Spider shell (*Lambis lambis*), 26
Spines, as weapons, 36
Spirobranchus gigantus, 27
Sponge(s), *15, 21, 26*
    Red Sea, 28-29
    as single-celled, 16
Staghorn coral, *17*
Starfish. *See* sea stars
Stinger cells, 34
Striped surgeonfish (*Acanthurus lineatus*), *30*
Subsidence, defined, 12
Suez fusiliers (*Caesia suevicus*), *2-3*
Sulfuric acid, 9
Swelling, as protective feature, 32
Swim bladder, function of, 38
Symbiosis, 18
    in reef life, *34-35*
Symphyllia sp., *21*
    madrepores as, 23
Synanceia verrucosa, *37*
Synanceiidae, 36

Tabular madrepore, *14*
Teeth, chitinous, 36, *37*
Tentacles, cnidarian's, 16
Terrace, *15*
Tethys Ocean, 12
Tetradontidae family, protective features of, 32
Thalassoma klunzingen, *31*
Theca(s), 12
    as connectors, 16
    described, 16
Thorns, as protective feature, 32
Thorny spine(s), sea urchin's, 34
Tidal channel, *15*
Tidal pools, as physiological "torture chamber," 26
Tide(s), influence of, 38
Tiger shark (*Galeocerdo cuvier*), *39*
    diet of, 39
Tree coral, *17*

Triassic Period, 12
Tridacna gigas, 24, 25, 26
Triggerfish, 29, *30, 31*
    jaws of, 32
Tropical rain forest:
    area of, 42, *48*
    destruction of, and coral reefs, 44
    land species on, 48-49
    living species in, *48-49*
Trumpetfish (*Aulostomus maculatus*), 3.
"Trunk," of radula, 36
Tube coral, *17*
Tunicates, as home for pearlfish, 32

United States, nuclear testing of, 46-47

Variola louti, 32
Viviparous, defined, 36
Volcanic activity, as required for coral reefs, 12

Warning signals, blackfin shark's, 38
Waste paper, 9
Waste products, damage wrought by, 9
Water:
    depth of, 14, 18, 40
    as H₂O, 18
    quality of, 18
    quality of, and coral reefs, 12
    recreational value of, 9
Weight:
    giant clam, 24
    hammerhead shark, 40
    Plectropomus maculatus, 29
Whale shark (*Rhincodon typus*), 38-40, *41*
Whip coral, *17*
Winds, direction of dominant, 15

Yellow arboreal gorgonia, 16
Yellow-masked angelfish (*Pomacanthus xanthometopon*), *30*
Yellow-striped triggerfish (*Balistapus undulatus*), *30*

Zanclidid, 32
Zanclus canescens, 32
Zebrasoma flaverscens, 32
Zooxanthellae:
    function of, 18
    symbiotic relationship of, with giant clam, 24
    symbiotic relationship of, with madrepores, *18*
    temperature of, 18
    temperature of, and coral reefs, 12

56

DATE DUE 03/01

MAY 1 0 2001	
JUN 0 4 2001	
SEP 0 7 2001	
OCT 0 5 2001	
JAN 0 3 2002	
FEB 0 9 2002	
JUN 1 7 2002	
DEC 0 3 2002	
NOV 1 7 2003	
OCT 2 3 2004	

GAYLORD   PRINTED IN U.S.A.